I0086663

QUIET MOMENTS

Writings, Poems, Wishes

Gary Gunsel

Copyright 2014 © by Gary H. Gunsel
All rights reserved including the right of reproduction of any part in
any form.

Design & Layout by Zach Gunsel

"The Red Gate" by Patsy Murphy

Published by The Boston Colored Easter Egg
San Rafael, CA.

ISBN-13:
978-0615965543 (The Boston Colored Easter Egg)

ISBN-10:
0615965547

To my wife, Patsy – my forever love and best friend.
Who taught me "all things are possible".

To my son, Zach – a true renaissance man.
He has revealed so much of life to me.

Several years ago I was diagnosed with prostate cancer—a definitive shock since I had always been an active and healthy person. The chaotic emotional responses were what you might expect—dread, fear and depression. The disease is the first thing you think about in the morning and the last thing you recall at night—and there is no place to hide.

The ensuing months only increased the anxiety with doctor appointments, tests and studying the various options of treatment (I chose surgery which subsequently was followed with radiation).

Certainly, blogs did not exist at that time but there are some words that I wrote a few months after the operation and I offer them here as a "blog" from the past. Like all quiet moments, I am hopeful that it provides an opportunity for reflection and a time for hope.

Looking back

One of my more emotional mornings so far with tears and expressions of fear and concern. I'm not sure how many more tears there might be but I suspect there are a few. I realize that, so far, there has not been a period of mourning for me—probably because of life's continuing quick pace and, also, because of the guilt I experience when I start to feel sorry of myself. It is always difficult to complain when I feel so very fortunate with what life has given me. Nevertheless, I sense that this may be a time for healthy tears and to work through a sorrow. I believe it will be positive and for the first time in months, I am experiencing some sense of calm—albeit subtle and in its infant stages.

I know that life will be different in the future but I now look at the prospect with more optimism and less fear. It may be that this "pause" that I have been given is a time to assess what has gone before and, more importantly, plan for changes in the future.

There are hurdles yet to overcome but I need to understand that there will always be hurdles and I need to remind myself that I have the strength to succeed and that I am blessed with Patsy and Zach to help me. For the first time in so many months, there seems to be a lightness of being.

Find your path.

Quiet Moments

At times, the world seems to be spinning much too quickly and seemingly with little sense of direction or purpose. It appears that we all seek a haven, a peaceful time when we are able to think and reflect and appreciate the life that we lead. It is a daunting and difficult task.

I started a blog a short time ago with the hope that I could contribute to the search for that haven—that peaceful time—that quiet moment. Make no mistake; there is no magical answer. As I have said before, "I am merely a pilgrim, like yourself" and still seeking.

This book is a compilation of those writings and, while there are no sudden epiphanies or enlightenments, there are some words of encouragement and some thoughts that you might ponder in your day-to-day life.

And please don't feel compelled to read these writings in order. Select any page you wish and I hope it will offer you a time for reflection.

I believe that taking a few minutes out of your schedule each day will allow you to discover the peace that you might have found to be elusive. If you look deeply into some of life's simplest offerings, you may just find a sense of relief and wellbeing. You may just find that quiet moment.

Writings

Hello and welcome to my little part of the universe—tucked away on the west coast but open to all who take the time to think, take the time to wonder and, most of all, take the time to try to find their way.

Make no mistake—I am not a preacher, guru or mystic. I am merely a pilgrim, like yourself, striving to make sense of my surrounding world and trying to recognize the joy and happiness that enters our lives everyday. It is not always easy to find—there are schedules to be kept, deadlines to be met and we all have demons that we must confront. But if you pause for a moment of stillness, the world will transform. Perhaps, only for that brief moment or, if you are fortunate, you will keep it with you for an hour or even longer or you may be able to lure it back into your consciousness later in the day.

Did you have your morning cup of coffee? Did you really taste how good it was, or was it just another daily ritual to be accomplished? Did you see, really see the magic of your surroundings or was the commute a blur—unseen because of a mind reeling with thoughts of the upcoming day?

My moment was watching steam rise off of the wet branches of a fir tree as the sun shone on it. Only a brief moment but a reaffirmation of the beauty that is in the world waiting to be seen.

And so the purpose of these words and, hopefully, more to come is to give you a moment of stillness that you may use as you see fit.

Knowing my nature, our meetings may be sporadic for I am less than timely with schedules. But I hope we connect again and that you will look for me. And I hope that I can be successful in gifting you with a quiet moment, even if only briefly.

Find your path.

A quiet moment—a quiet moment—did you find yours today. Difficult isn't it? Sometimes, nearly impossible. Our world doesn't always lend itself easily to quietude and peace and we are buffeted by winds of uncertainty, anxiety and fear. Maybe the answer is closing yourself off to it but do we really want to be a hermit or a recluse, run away from the formidable challenges that we face daily and hope to find that elusive tranquility?

Staying in the world, in the present moment is important. Thich Nhat Hanh referred to it as "engaged Buddhism"—being always available but attempting to find that "center" within ourselves—that quiet place that remains undisturbed by the maelstrom of everyday life. Believe me, I'm not saying it's easy and I am probably more guilty than most in losing my way when I struggle to find my center. But I keep trying and I am hopeful that you keep trying too. It is a moment-to-moment game but the rewards are there—subtle but always there.

For today, I realize that a quiet moment for me is writing these words and hoping there are those who will find some value in them. I know that we don't all have the luxury of taking this kind of "time out" but, perhaps, you could start with just a minute or maybe two and look within for the peace that is always there. It makes all the difference that you keep searching.

Find your path.

Not all quiet moments are pleasant ones. Some carry pain and can be disheartening and life altering.

I had such a moment several days ago when my sister, Barb, called to tell me that her son, Mike, had succumbed to the cancer that had ravaged his body for several months. Mike had undergone so many treatments but the disease can be unforgiving and continued to spread. So the phone call was not unexpected but piercingly painful nonetheless. And, as Barb and I talked over the next hour or so, we tried to make some sense of this tragedy and, in a way, make sense of how and why the world turns as it does.

There are not answers, of course, only questions to be pondered and philosophies to be considered. It does not shake my faith but it alters my being and reinforces the fragility of life that we see but don't often want to recognize.

After we hung up, I spent quite a bit of time alone and, yes, they were quiet moments but gave no solace—only more questions.

I wish I could understand. I wish I could make sense of the life we lead. I sometimes think that the wiser I become, the less I comprehend. But there is no choice for any of us, only the mandate to keep searching.

Find your path.

I had my quiet moment this morning when I talked with my best friend and she reminded me that trying to control outside forces only leads to frustration and a loss of true self. In all likelihood, there is only a small corner of the universe that we have any control over whatsoever, and it is us. We can begin each day with a "clean slate" and decide what presence we will bring to it. We can choose happiness and contemplation and joy. And, best of all, we can infuse those same feelings with each being that we encounter during the day. To quote Ram Dass, "the best thing I can do for you is work on me".

Believe me, I don't mean to make this sound easy and effortless—it's not. Every day we are bombarded with agonizing news and painful reports. And I'm not saying just give up and not to try to change the wrongs that you encounter. But I am saying not to let it be your master; don't let it change who you are and who you are meant to be.

We can work on ourselves constantly and consistently and change is bound to occur. It may not be on the grand scale that we would like and it may not happen as quickly as we would like, but it will make a difference. Each of us can be a contributor.

I know if I watch the news tonight it will provide the same litany of hurt, anger and broken dreams. But thanks to the wisdom of my best friend, I remember the choices that I can make, and I will do so.

I wish you the same.

Find your path.

I realized today that quiet moments do not always spring into your consciousness—sometimes they evolve. Earlier, I was fortunate to be outside and see an array of large puffy clouds slowly easing their way across the morning sky. It was almost startling and, of course, the irony is that they are there many times—not every day to be sure—but many times. But today I was conscious of them and marveled at their beauty—a moment of recognition but not necessarily a quiet moment in itself. That came later.

I traced the clouds' movements over the next hour or so, watching them change shape, disappear and be replaced by others. And, of course, the age old "revelation" dawned on me—we are all living under that same beautiful sky and my quiet moment evolved. There was a confirmation of sorts that, regardless of the strife, hardships and difficulties, we are united under one sky. And I gently hoped that this unification could, in some way, manifest a recognition of unity of mankind. No, I am not naïve enough to think the world's problems will suddenly fade. I only continue to hope that we each try to work on ourselves and those we meet, and believe that we will create a more peaceful planet.

Find your path.

In the front yard the Japanese Maple is just beginning to sprout miniature leaves and flowers are showing the first signs of blooms. It is a reminder of the consistency of nature and of its continuing beauty. A quiet moment of observation, but also, a lesson that the peacefulness of this pageant marches ahead regardless of the sometimes chaotic conditions that exist. They endure storms, cold and climate change but nature perseveres.

Are we able to do the same? It is, perhaps, why we continue to search for that quiet moment—an anchor that grounds us amid the day-to-day challenges. There is no way to stop the spinning of the world and the worries that seem to pervade our consciousness. But like nature, we can persevere and we can continue to bloom. And we can, one by one, try to persuade others to do the same.

Try to take the time to look at nature today, whether it be tree, flower or the hummingbird that darts across the landscape. If you can't find them nearby, close your eyes for a moment or two and imagine them. Listen to the lessons they tacitly impart. You and I must strive for peace of mind and for the greater peace that needs healing. If not us, who?

Find your path.

No, I cannot define the word nor can I explain what it means to anyone but myself. And, even then, it has so many nuances that I am convinced we must just accept that love is the most powerful and precious emotion that we will ever know. And, I believe, that love creates more quiet moments than any force we will ever encounter.

This past weekend my wife and son took me to dinner to celebrate my birthday and as we sat in the restaurant, I looked at the two most loved people in my life and thought of how fortunate I am. And I was able to experience my quiet moment amidst the bustle and noise of a hundred diners; love does that. And I feel so blessed because the moment recurred again and again over the weekend. And each time it calmed my soul and reminded me of the sacredness of my life.

I hope that love touches everyone in some way. It is a means to the salvation of our lives. In a world that sometimes seems to be immersed in chaos and conflict (if you believe the media), love is the antidote. And if you try to find that quiet moment, I believe you will find love in your life. And, no, it does not always mean romantic; there are so many sources of love, whether it be close friends, pets, a walk in nature or so many other possibilities. Love covers a very large territory.

When you have time for that quiet moment, reflect on the love that exists in your life in one form or another and it will touch your heart.

I wish you love.

Find your path

Since I have been looking out my window at the rain for the past half hour, it seems like an appropriate quiet moment to consider. It is my good fortune that this is the type of rain that lends itself to contemplation—falling steadily but not windswept and blustery (although the wind seems to be picking up as I write these words).

I realize that we are not all fans of the rain. I have been known to rant at it more than a few times. But there are so many times when it is the perfect opportunity to sit and be still, to find that quiet moment and be thankful for the grace that nature bestows upon us. We can turn inward and allow thoughts and ideas to cross the landscape of our minds without interruption and intrusion (if we are lucky).

When I was younger and running was my daily habit, I welcomed the rainy days and made sure that I always jogged three or four miles through the storm. I undoubtedly felt that it was a "badge of honor". These years later, I still don't mind a short walk through the drops but I suspect that I lean more toward just what I am doing today—admiring the peaceful rainfall through my window and thinking how lovely some flames might look in the fireplace.

I suppose the point of all this is the calmness and serenity that are possible when we take the time to observe what nature offers us and use it as a pathway to be still and thoughtful. I hope you find that quiet moment today.

Find your path.

I am a most fortunate person because my day begins in the company of my best friend—my wife. And the quiet moment it presents to me is the time we have together at our breakfast table. I know it sounds a bit ordinary but, like so many things in our lives, it becomes special because of the recognition that we bring to it. No, it's not unlike the morning meals that millions of people share every day—coffee, tea and a bite to eat—but it gives me a quiet moment to reflect on my life and the amazing grace I have been given in finding my lifetime love. And it quiets my mind and provides me with the peace to prepare for the day ahead.

Certainly, all of us have different situations and we each must find our own way to create stillness to sustain us through the day. The point is, what better time is there to find your quiet moment than at the beginning of the day? It is a matter of taking a minute or two, being quiet and aware, and recognizing what is good in your life and how it will prepare you for the day. I don't mean to make it sound easy—it's not. It is a challenge to quiet your mind and difficult to focus on calmness. But trying each day brings it closer.

I hope your day is peaceful and that there are quiet moments to be found.

Find your path.

I called a college friend yesterday. I have not seen or spoken to him in about five years. He and I have been good friends for many years but like so many instances, the pace of life creates vacuums and we lose touch totally without meaning to—"we'll call tomorrow"—and it is that tomorrow that tends not to arrive for a long time.

My quiet moment came shortly after we hung up. I realized that "no time had passed"—we were still the same friends that we had been for so long. We are meeting within a week or so and, while I'm sure that our physical beings have changed just a bit, we are still the same two people and the relationship maintains.

It is a quiet moment of awareness. Life continues—sometimes at a pace that seems much too rapid. But, fortunately, there are also enduring truths and, if we are lucky, friendship is one of them.

Perhaps you may want to contact that friend you haven't seen for a little while and discover a quiet moment yourself.

Find your path.

"If we could see the miracle of a single flower clearly, our whole life would change".

Yes, I wish I had written those words but the author is Siddhartha Gautama, better known as Buddha. But isn't it the perfect reflection of quiet moments removed from life's daily turmoil and immersed in the present beauty of the world that surrounds us? How deeply can we observe our landscape and how much time can we devote to it?

Certainly, in this world we have created, there are few if any of us who could have the luxury of hours of reflection (or mediation) let alone sit under the Bodhi tree for days as Buddha did. So we must be as conscious as possible to find one or two quiet moments and use them as conscientiously as possible. Can you spare a minute or two at lunch to sit in a quiet space (not a cubicle)? Are you able to come home after work and sit, just sit for your peace of mind? I'm not lecturing here—I find it as difficult as you probably do to sit still. But the more I try it, the easier it becomes. And life takes on a different perspective.

I still remember when I was much younger (early twenties, I believe) looking at a blade of grass for what seemed like hours (I suspect ten or fifteen minutes). But it was extraordinary. As I examined the intricacies of this creation, I was in awe, not only of its incredible beauty but, also, the complexity of it. And I thought of Walt Whitman—"to see the world in a blade of grass"—and realized the possibilities.

Today, try to take that quiet moment. It makes all the difference.

Find your path.

There is no compromise for me; first and foremost in my life is my family. I have been graciously blessed with a wife and son and they have completed my being in ways that I never imagined. And they are responsible for so many quiet moments in my daily living—moments when I can reflect on the love we share in so many ways and the privilege it is to be a part of this magical circle. It emphasizes the good fortune that I have experienced and taught me not to take life for granted. It is precious and doesn't necessarily come easily. It needs to be nurtured and vigilantly protected.

When you can, take a moment—a quiet moment—and give thanks for your family in whatever form it takes. There are so many ways in which we form families and, of course, all are different. If we are lucky, there is a common thread of love—not always easy to recognize and not always easy to maintain—but, hopefully, it is there.

Then, of course, there is the extended family of our world. Try to give a quiet moment to them also; there is no doubt that we need it.

I hope you take a moment today and I hope your family is well.

Find your path.

As I've added years, I have probably grown less fond of crowds. Perhaps it is because of the media and the unruly rampages that they tend to feature as their lead stories. More likely, however, it is my own evolution to a more solitary being than I used to be. It's not that I am a loner— far from it—I enjoy being with people and would consider myself a social being. I think it's just that I have come to prefer smaller groups.

And all of this started me thinking of the quiet moments that come in crowds of all sizes. I sometimes think that we wait to experience our quiet moments in times of meditation or at least solitude. But the truth is that moments of awareness happen anytime and anywhere if we are attentive. I know that I have had the experience of an unexpected encounter with a total stranger in a crowded situation (elevator, street corner, etc) and I believe that there seems to be an instant connection. I suspect that you may have had the same experience. It is unlikely that there will be any kind of following relationship but for that moment during a conversation of perhaps no more than 20 words, there is a quiet moment— one that you will probably reflect on later. And there is a feeling that the world is not quite as chaotic as we might think; there are moments that we connect on another level. And it gives us a glimmer of a higher understanding.

I hope you have your quiet moment today. It could be anywhere at anytime.

Find your path.

I feel certain that all of us would like to be optimists, thinking the best of the world and those who populate it. Not always easy, is it? Each day we filter through bewildering news events, being cut off in traffic, arriving late for an appointment and so many other disturbing happenings that it is sometimes so difficult to keep our smile in its place. And, at times, there is an element of panic because we feel helpless to change the circumstances. Perhaps, that is the problem because the cruel fact is that we cannot alter the world. The good news is that we do have control over our little corner of the world, because we decide how we react to our surroundings. It is a conscious decision, but like so many things, not always easy.

My best friend has always told me that "all things are possible" and it is absolutely true. And she is a shining example because she believes in the goodness of our world—she sees the positive side of nature. And, thankfully, she has helped me toward this same outlook. No, I'm not always successful but I do keep trying and in my moments of pessimism or, worse yet, depression, I try to remember I have the power to change my view of the world.

If you have not read Desiderata (Max Ehrmann), you should take the time (about 3 minutes) to do so. Some of the closing words are "with all its sham, drudgery and broken dreams, it is still a beautiful world". There are so many quiet moments to be found in this prose poem and it poses more philosophical questions than we could ever hope to mention in our few paragraphs. But the crux is that we must accept the world on its terms; it is our reaction that can work miracles.

Find your path.

Outside of immediate family, friendships are some of the most important relationships we develop. They are unique in their substance, ranging from close friends with whom you share your life to acquaintances that are friends but, perhaps, seen infrequently.

I feel fortunate (perhaps a better word is blessed) that I have had incredible friendships through my life. I hope you have experienced the same. The relationships they represent are a critical part of our lives and our humanity. And over the years, I have learned some valuable insights about the spectrum of emotions friends evoke.

One of the most important came a few years ago when my wife and I were lucky enough to take a bike tour in Italy. To this day, I consider it one of the best if not the best vacation we have ever experienced. There is little to find fault with when you are spoiled by beautiful countryside, remarkable food and amazing wines. And, of course, the great aspect of biking everyday, so the poundage you gain is minimal.

But one of the best rewards was the group of people with whom we shared this journey. For five days we were the closest of friends sharing our stories and our lives and, of course, at the end of the trip, we exchanged contact information, promising to stay in touch.

I think we have all experienced times like this and we know deep in our hearts how unlikely it is that the relationships will endure. But I've learned, the continuance of the friendship is not the important point. I have had so many quiet moments over the years evoking the memories of those "friends" and the warmth of our days together. And it has taught me that momentary friends can have incredible influences on our lives.

So now in my daily interactions, I try to make "friends" with those that I meet, knowing it is fleeting but also realizing that many of them will bring me quiet moments along the way. I hope you have a quiet moment with a "friend" that you meet today.

Find your path.

No, I'm not speaking of Ben & Jerry or Hewlett Packard but of the partnership formed by the intimacy between two people. I suppose I could have said "significant other" but it sounded a bit stilted and, of course, "marriage" also would not work because of the evolving definitions in our society. I'm a bit old fashioned (perhaps just old) but I am a fan of marriage but I also understand that this relationship is not always legally possible. And so we move ahead with partnership as the word of choice.

And, you might ask, "where does this lead us to quiet moments"? The transition is an easy and natural one. Where is there a more meaningful moment than thinking of your partner and taking time to contemplate how your life has been blessed by the relationship. You should never let a day pass without feeling that gratitude; life has given you a precious gift.

When my wife and I married, our wedding bands were inscribed "To my friend" and these years later, it is still the strength of our love. We are friends in a partnership.

I hope you take time today to think of your partner—a quiet moment to hold that person close. If you are still seeking that partner, then I hope the time is not far off and, perhaps, you can still have a quiet moment to contemplate the possibilities that undoubtedly lie ahead.

It only takes a moment.

Find your path.

For the past several minutes, I have been staring out our window where we are fortunate enough to have a vista of one of California's most majestic mountains. It is a scene I have grown used to in the past 14 years that we have lived in this house, but I never grow tired of the view and I never take it for granted—I know how lucky I am. Today, the mountain, as usual, brings me peace of mind and, perhaps, more importantly, a sense of timelessness. In my humble human thinking, the mountain has existed forever and will continue its vigil farther into the future than I am capable of comprehending. It is eternal.

I don't always "wax poetic" and I don't always take the time to really appreciate the magnificence of this view. But taking those minutes today reaped the reward of awareness and that is really what "quiet moments" is all about. In our world of "24/7" with uninterrupted intrusions, it is a daunting task to find the time—that moment—to absorb the beauty around us. And, of course, the irony is that it is always there waiting for our recognition. Time is the joker.

Today, in your maelstrom of tasks, errands and appointments, try to find that time (that "quiet moment", if you will) to embrace some beauty and peace in your surroundings. It may not always be easy to identify, but I believe you can find it. Just take a little time.

Find your path.

Of all the quiet moments, I have to believe that the most meaningful ones involve love. Love in all its forms and variations.

Quite some time ago, Patsy and I decided that we would celebrate our 30th wedding anniversary by renewing our vows of marriage in a small ceremony with the two of us and our incredible son, Zach. We chose one our favorite vacation spots farther up the coast and were rewarded with one of the most beautiful houses imaginable with ocean vistas that were—to use a cliché—breathtaking. Standing on the deck we could look left to the beach and see seven sea lion pups with their moms and if we looked up to the right we were fortunate on the first day to see an osprey that stood majestically on a tree branch for hours.

On our original invitations in 1982, we said, "on this day I will marry my friend" and in all these 30 years, this has never wavered, only grown more precious. We used the statements and vows that we had written those many years ago and we recreated the bouquet and the flower wreath that graced Patsy's head. And I swear that she radiated the same beauty of our wedding day. Zach coordinated our ritual, took pictures and closed the ceremony with one of the most poignant poems that I have heard. It was a day that has changed our hearts forever. Love does that.

Yes, I feel most fortunate. It is a quiet moment that I will carry and treasure always.

I wish that love finds its way to everyone; it is what makes life vibrant and gives it meaning. And it is everywhere if we seek it. During your quiet times today, mediate on love and I think you might be surprised how often you encounter it. Maybe not always romantic but love has many incarnations. May it touch you today.

Find your path.

Sometimes I feel weary—not despaired—but tired.
The headlines pierce your eyes
And the world seems plunged into chaos.
And there seem to be no answers
Only questions asking other questions.
I cannot decipher the darkness in our society
But I know they are the actions of few.
And we seek solace in some corner of our mind
Some corner of our heart.
I am sustained by my family
A wife and son who bring love and light into my life.
And it makes me certain of the goodness of the world.
And I face each day holding them close to my heart
And I am at peace.
There is beauty everywhere, waiting to be seen.

Find your path.

Looking across the restaurant table,
I see your beauty so clearly
And I realize there is no need for words at this moment.
Only you and me and the love that we have bonded over
these many years.

And it always makes me wonder when I notice other
wordless couples

Have they exhausted their verbal discourse
Or, like us, are they blessed with moments that say so very
much without words.

I am doubly fortunate
Because I dearly love our discussions – our philosophizing
into the nights,
"solving the world's problems" and visioning future steps
of our life together
our love only grows stronger.

But the quiet moments – they also touch my heart
And I am so content to be with you in the moment

Wordless – but saying so much.

Find your path.

"To love another person is to see the face of God". Yes, we saw Les Mis several days ago (the 25th anniversary, if you can believe it) and it is still inspiring and stirs the soul. And the finale with the above words truly stops the heart and the breath and you are taken to a place where you want to grope your way to understanding the world and the people in it. I mean, seeing the face of God is pretty heady stuff, just as is loving another person and it awes you to the point of trying to get a glimpse, however small, of the miracle of life. You know, that miracle that pervades our lives everyday but rarely catches our attention. In between the errands, chores, work and 24/7 technology, there seems little time just to quiet our minds and contemplate how extraordinary life really is, how blessed we are to exist on this spinning globe in the vastness of the universe.

Can you take that "quiet moment" today? Can you find the stillness to reflect on life and your place in the grand scheme of our spirit? Yes, it's more difficult than it seems and, while I've failed so many times, I'm still trying.

I have seen the face of God. I cannot tell you what she/he looks like but in loving another person, my heart has visualized the image and, like so many revelations, one is never the same.

Wordsworth said, "to me the meanest flower that blows can give thoughts that do often lie too deep for tears"—another opportunity for contemplation.

Try to find that "quiet moment" today. The insights could be extraordinary.

Just a thought.

Find your path.

My everyday interactions with people have undergone changes and transitions over the past several years. And while I might be considered somewhat on the introspective side, I usually am a fairly outgoing personality, given to starting conversations with "strangers"—folks in the grocery line, clerks, delivery people—almost anyone. And the past years have increased this propensity; as I have aged, I have become less reserved (perhaps, less afraid) in making these daily contacts. I converse, shake hands, touch arms—all within my comfort zone. They are all quiet moments (except with words) and reward me with renewed faith in those with whom I share this daily life. And I am always intrigued by the welcoming response from my "fellow travelers"—it is as if they hunger for contact in what has become a more sterile technological world. And while we both know that it is a passing moment between "strangers" who are not likely to meet again, it is recognition of the goodness that exists among our tribe of humans—a spiritual union.

"Namaste"—a worldwide greeting, usually meaning, "I bow to you" or "I salute the light within you". Or, as Ram Dass explains it, "if you are in that place in you, and I am in that place in me, there is only one of us".

Total strangers—I have come to believe that they don't exist.

During your travels today, say hello to someone you've never met. I promise it won't hurt.

Find you path.

"Were you ever out in the great alone when the moon was awful clear?
And the icy mountains hemmed you in with a silence you most could hear?"
Poetry of Robert Service.

Sometimes, there is a "Sound of Silence". And for most of us, that silence is so different, so removed from our daily life that it is almost startling. And, yet, don't we all seek that "quiet moment", that time when life seems to go on pause for just the briefest of times? And if we are lucky enough to find that time and are alert and listen intently, we find a meaningful chance for reflection.

I wish that I meditated more, fully aware that I am at fault. But sometimes, I think we give meditation too formal a meaning. There are times when we can just sit and let our spirit float through thoughts and scenarios of the day. No, it's not counting breaths, not trying to rid the mind of earthly ideas. But it is, I believe, just as rewarding and we can truly feel the refreshment of this "quiet moment" with ourselves.

I would like to have more answers to share but, as I said before, I am just a pilgrim, like you, trying to find my way, my path. But I do know that if you have the fortune of finding a peaceful place to enjoy for a few moments and listen to the quiet intently, you will sense a hint of transformation. And that is a beginning.

Find your path.

Sometimes quiet moments are only in your mind and in your heart while the world outside is chaotic and loud. For me, last evening was such a time.

It was the opening ceremonies for the second game of the World Series and in honor of our armed forces, a marine was chosen to deliver the ceremonial first pitch. However, this young man is a triple amputee and walking stiffly with a cane, he made his way to the pitcher's mound with Barry Zito, a San Francisco pitcher beside him, hand on his shoulder. Zito held the cane and the marine threw his pitch with 50,000 baseball fans cheering louder than you can imagine. But for me, it was quiet and I suspect, from the look on his face, it was quiet for the soldier as well. He had a glowing smile filled with joy and, yes, a quiet dignity.

I will never understand mankind's violence and hatred and the seemingly endless wars that plague our planet. And I am reminded of a Rod McKuen song that includes the words "it makes me cry to see the things some men do to one another". And I cried too last night but the tears were not sad but hopeful. For me, the marine represents bravery of incredible magnitude. Not because of his combat experience but because of his spirit in the face of such tragic aftermath. And in an unusual way, it is an inspiration of hope that mankind will prevail even under dire circumstances.

It was a quiet moment of reflection and a vision that humanity still has a chance to be human.

Find your path.

The rain is falling steadily but quietly right now and I am fortunate enough to be inside. It induces a feeling of calmness, almost serenity. Fortunate is a word I have thought about over the past several days and it touches me in so many ways with so many meanings. But the headlines that have blazed across most newspapers and the lead story that has dominated the airways recently have served to remind me of the most important way that I am fortunate. I am a "family man", blessed with a lovely and loving wife and a kind and thoughtful son. It has been a "long term" relationship and I am trusting that it will endure for quite some time more. Clint Black wrote a song with the words, "When I said I do, I meant that I will till the end of all time". And that is how it should be.

Trust me, I am not about to preach about morality; it's not my place to do so and, goodness knows, my past is certainly not without its errors. But the web of intrigue that has been exposed has given unprecedented publicity to extramarital affairs at the highest levels of the military. And, no, it is not for me to pass judgment or condemn anyone. I am only left with a feeling of sadness, a feeling of loss for all of the people involved and the pain that has been inflicted and will continue to haunt them.

"Power corrupts"—it is a quote from over one hundred years ago. Does it apply to this situation? Maybe. But we all understand that it is not only the powerful that fall prey to these mistakes. It's just that, in this case, names, pictures and sordid details are fodder for the media.

Is there a quiet moment here? For me there is. Sadly, it might be selfish—I hope not—but I think of my life and my family and the joy that has blessed us all these years. And I think of the word.

Fortunate. Fortunate.

Find your path.

It always seems like the holidays keep us in some sort of suspended animation, or perhaps that's just me. At any rate, the holidays were lovely and, goodness knows, there were so many quiet moments. I just suffered from writer's block and didn't seem able to express the precious moments that I experienced.

That being said, life moves ahead and I muddle my way through, groping for words that I somehow hope will have meaning. And, in some ways, that itself is a quiet moment. There is a gentle peace when writing if, for no other reason, than it is a solitary time for reflection and introspection. And, if I am honest, I find it more in poetry and believe that it is the most truthful expression of the human condition.

I have been mentoring several high school students for the past few months with my "specialty" being English. And, yes, we have covered the basic groundwork of grammar, punctuation, vocabulary, etc. But, at some point, our meetings took on more of a general tone and, oddly enough, poetry became a focal point. And I was pleasantly surprised to find that there was interest in and curiosity of poetic expression. Somehow it is reaffirming to see young people gravitate to poetry but, also, interesting that they have no reservations about expressing their enjoyment of it. And so, over the past few weeks, we have explored the world of poets both old and modern—even to the point that I asked them to memorize one and they embraced the "assignment".

How long has it been since you read a poem? How long since you memorized one? Would you like an "assignment" too?

I promise it will be rewarding and believe that it might even work its way into your daily life. And, trust me, it will lead you to quiet moments.

Find your path.

On some distant day, I'll find answers to eternal questions.
And, perhaps, the world will make perfect sense
and my place in it will slide into being.
As it is, I still grope for understanding
To comprehend what sometimes seems chaotic
And to strive for elusive conclusions.
The mistake, of course, is forgetting that the search
Is the answer – is the knowing – is the belief.
Taking time to sit in the stillness brings the perspective to life
And a calmness that settles questions – and answers.
We all hurry too much – worry too much
When, as the Taoists say, "all is done without doing".
I hope there is stillness in your life today
And in mine.
All is as it should be.

Find your path.

Wisdom—such a highly charged word, subject to so many nuances and interpretations. Too often equated with intelligence, but in reality, so very different. To be wise you may not be intelligent and, of course, vice versa. Perhaps, you are fortunate to possess both qualities. Only you know.

Am I wise? I desperately hope so but, perhaps, the jury is still out on that decision. But this I do know—I am wiser now than I used to be. And, no, I do not necessarily believe it to be a part of the aging process (although I'm sure it helps) but more a reflection of the quiet moments that we try to make part of our lives. Times of introspection that clarify who we are and how we relate to this life we are blessed to be living.

I am aware of the tremendous chaos that confronts us everyday from so many sources. The news seems to bludgeon us constantly with tragedies and tries to weaken our belief in humankind. And, yes, I am so outraged by the inhumanity we encounter that the anger seethes in my being and my sense of justice and retribution threaten to smother my nature of compassion. I'm afraid it is a daily battle.

But, over the years, I have found solace in the understanding that for every act of atrocity, there are thousands of wonders occurring all around us. Somewhere, there is a beautiful song being written, there is a heartfelt poem being penned and there are acts of kindness being traded from one human being to another. We are still a race of loving entities—lost sometimes, but never surrendering to the darkness.

Take time today (and everyday) to calm your mind and focus your senses to the miracles that are a part of your life. You may be surprised at just how many wondrous moments there are.

I wish you (and me) wisdom and understanding.

Find your path.

Poems and Wishes

I glance at my watch
And think – maybe, maybe
And I know I can't
But if I could, I'd stop time
Here on this Northern California beach
That smells of morning
And we could stay children for
Just a moment longer,
Leaving deadlines and projects
And tedium
In their place – away from us.
While we dream dreams
And plan escapes
And look within
For the peace that is always there
Yet stays elusive,
Close enough to touch
But only for moments
Here and there.
Let's walk back
And see our seals
Sunning on the rocks
One more time.
The leaving will come soon enough
But the drive home will be gentler
Because you're with me.

As always,
Fall comes more quickly than I imagine
And sooner than I expect.
And, once again,
The melancholy will squeeze my heart
Ever so slightly
The ache will return
As will the longing that
Has no direction
No returning home
As if home might still be there.
Do they still have leaf piles?
The ones you lie in
With the musky smell of earth
All about you.
The factories still belch poisons into the sky
But, God, I'll never smell a burning leaf again.
The fluorescent colors will continue to startle my eyes
And I will forever try to complete myself
In this season of forgiving and twilight.
I'll know when it is time to go home again
And fall will be the reminder.

For just a moment
I thought I saw your bear
Peeking out from your backpack
But, no, it was your laptop
And you were off to college
Not to day care.
And I am left alone in the Oakland Airport
To wonder how – how did you become a man
So very quickly
When did I have to reach up just to hug you
And how did this hand that I held just a moment ago
become larger than mine.
There is no sense of loss,
Only a vague regret
Of somehow not being able to hold
Each precious moment just a little longer.
I got lost somewhere between
Mario Bros and iPod
And you kept going
As you should.
I'd like to think you'll come back
But I know that time only moves forward
And on each return you will be different
And, of course, I would not change it
It is as it should be
And as much as I loved that
Little boy for oh so many years,
I love my son even more.

The world embraces me and holds me close
It opens my eyes to beauty and my ears to symphonies
The natural unfolding of a potential that we need to grasp
      And you are here.

And there are times when clouds gather on the horizon
When we are challenged by twilight or darkness
And we struggle to comprehend and to face the unknown
      But you are here.

You are here – in my arms, in my thoughts and my
prayers
But most of all – always in my heart.
You are here – a lover, a best friend, a spiritual support
And a guide to keep me from losing my way.
You are here for this day and an eternity of days.

And the world spirals through its path
The ebb and flow of life weaves its unchartered seas
And I awaken to the beauty that is my life
      And you're here.

Will you walk with me
Will you love me
Will you place your hand with mine

Yesterday was like that
As we reveled in a perfect Sausalito day.
An ideal sun in a surrealistic blue sky
It should have been hotter
But
The fog prowled under the Golden Gate
So the breezes were warm with comfort
And kissed us ever so lightly.

And we paused to sit and marvel
At the so familiar panorama
The bridge, the rocks, the bay water – even the tour buses.
It is always so recognizable and always so new.
And as we sat together I realized the same is true for us
Always so recognizable and always so new.
Our love grows in ways that continue to astound me
Each day
Each moment
But it is still "just us" and that will never change.

As we walked back to the car
We held hands
And I realized it is so natural
That I am sometimes not aware
Exactly when we slip our hands together.

Will you walk with me
Will you love me
Will you place your hand with mine

Trust me, I know how hard it is to believe
How hard it is to keep the tired heart from surrender
And how hard it is, day after day, to face what has become
a surrealistic landscape.
There is no escape.
The headlines sear our eyes, TV and radio assault our
senses
Even the Internet has joined this most improbable circus
of human folly.

But it is imperative that you resist,
Rise above it so you can see the truth
Recognize these shadows for what they truly are
A camouflage to beauty and goodness
A specter trying to hide love and caring.
You must pause, lock out the noise and look more deeply
You will see, you will see what you always knew was there.

Squirrels scamper frantically across limbs
Jays issue their piercing caws to one another
Flowers bloom, plants grow
And the trees dance slowly with the mild warm breezes.
And people?
If you look closely you will see hand holding, kissing
And the exchange of loving glances, sometimes, even
words.
Today (and every day) we will be out there helping one
another
We will (sometimes against the odds) be fighting for
someone's dignity
It may even be our own.

And me??
"guilty as charged, your honor" – I didn't always see the
world,
Only the shadows.
And I would say, "the wiser I become, the less I
understand."
True enough but...

What I didn't realize is the less I understand
The more I have to believe.
And as I have taken those first tentative steps
The world has been kind enough to open.

Where is my innocence?
There is an echo from, oh, so long ago
Faint but thank God, still audible.
Somewhere on a side road – a path I used to walk
And now uncharted with no map home.
But when I am aware – when I live in the moment
I stumble with those first tentative steps
Toward that familiar land where I've never been.
And they're waiting for me there,
The real make-believe friends
That peopled my life so long ago.
And during those brief moments
Of recognition
I wonder not how
But why
Did I ever leave?

I am an angel without wings.
No one's fault really,
Maybe mine but I hope not.
I recognize the familiar landscape
Still littered with good intentions
With unfulfilled deeds.
I could have
I should have
I will
Maybe next week when I have more time.
It's possible,
If only I had the power, the wings.
And so
We all flail
Shout to the furies
Protest to the fates
And wait.
Wait for the wings
For the chance
For the promise to manifest.
At moments I feel so very close.
Sometimes I reach out
And I swear I can cradle it in my arms.
Still, it's elusive,
Keeping a distance
But staying in sight.
Perhaps, to tell me it's still possible.
But for now
I am an angel without wings.

I know that somewhere there was a past
Days when I was young, when I chased love
Or at least someone to ease my night into morning.
Sometimes I found pretenders, substitutes for love,
And maybe they loved me
But, really, I was never sure,
And was never sure that it mattered,
God, sometimes I'm not even sure it really happened.
There's only this day with you
And the fate that led up to it
And the forever that follows.

And all of it with you.
How could it be anything else?
Where else would I go?
Somehow it always,
Always led to you
And I knew it
In the way we know the god that dwells within
But never really see him,
Never really see the purpose, the design
But know that everything fits
That it unfolds exactly as it should.

Tomorrow is tomorrow
Nothing else
But it's a day with you
Another day of "us".
And I feel no guilt, no sense of greed
In wanting it...
And more.

Late spring – slowly but ever so steadily turning to summer
The signs are all about us
Trees are leafed in green
The bird symphony awakens us an hour earlier than
desired
Buds turn to radiant blooms
And the breezes touch your cheek ever so softly with
warmth.

It is a ritual transition whose meanings change with the
march of years.
Not so long ago (at least in my mind) it was a sign of
release
Three months of vacation and, perhaps, my greatest chore
Was oiling a baseball glove for the season
Making sure that I arrived at the playground promptly
each day.

It seems so very distant now and, somehow, far less
distinctive.

Over the recent years,
The foray into the summer season brings joy in so many
other ways
Days wrapped in a pleasant warmth
Evenings sparkling with sunlight as the days lengthen
And weather that invites both exciting movement or, at
times, cozy laziness.

But, mostly, it is you.
My thoughts turn to you and our time together
Our walks down familiar trails – holding hands (and no
jackets)
Bike rides for lattes with the ever present decision
Of what path we should ride next.
And, of course, "Italian picnics" by our beloved rock
Easing the afternoon into early evening.

I hope you know you are all of my seasons

You are the reason for my autumn, winter, spring and summer.
And, as each season moves to the next,
It reminds me of how much and in how many ways
I love you.
Happy summer, my pretty lady.

God knows where I might have gone
What I might have done
How lost I might have been
If I hadn't seen that face, that day
"across a crowded room".

But I did
and there was no way that it couldn't happen
there are events that have a surety to them
a force so strong that the world bows with understanding.

And, now, thirty-three Christmases later
I am so fortunate to look across the room
And still see that angel and that smile that undoes my heart
Still realize that I have been blessed with love
That has no boundaries, no limits and defies to be
described by words.
"I see you".

Merry Christmas, my princess.
I love you so.

Love,
g

What is it about fathers and sons that stirs the mind – and
the heart,
Each relationship different.

Males grope for intimacy with difficulty.
Looking for appropriate affection
While trying still to "be a man" – whatever that means.
Affection is so easy with our "baby boys"
Sometimes more tedious as the years push on.

And so I recognize how fortunate and privileged I am
That you are my son.
Over all these years, it has always been so easy
To respect you, to admire you and, of course, to love you.
Being your dad has given dimension to my life
And filled my heart.

So, my son, Merry Christmas.
Just wanted you to know – I love you
On this Christmas Day and always.

Love,
d

Your voice sounds just a bit older – barely noticeable but
still evident
And, of course, when I look in the mirror I know why.
The songs are the same but the interpretation so different.
Is it wrong – is it less than it should be?
No – rather an aging that so reflects where we've gone
Not only you – but all of us.
It has been a graceful trip
Not without its pain
But so much worth the journey.
And the perspective?
I really don't know.
I'd like to think that there's a wisdom
A knowledge that's worth all the battles
But there are moments when it all seems futile
That I'll never reach understanding
Never see what should be so obvious.
But year follows year (sometimes so quickly that I tremble)
And I know that the answer is so simple.
Just stop – stop and be in the moment.
Listen to your song and appreciate your voice
For where it's been and where it is
And, of course, I understand.
It is the universal song that is never the same.
It is our life – then and now
And the magic and beauty that happened on the way.
And, answer of answers, the miracles yet to be
As we struggle to our future.

Where do I start?
With love, perhaps
Always a good place.
In some small way it was expected, wanted, needed
Thought about on so may nights in so many lonely places.
But nothing like this
So much more than anticipated
And, God help me, more than I deserve
More than I have earned
More than I can ever repay.
Is there a love debt?
What do I do for the rest of my life?
And beyond?
To make up for this?
God knows – I'll try,
The frailty will haunt me
But I'm still strong and I still believe,
I'll work on me and I'll help you.
It's all there is
All I can do.

You are across the room – reclining softly on the sofa
And cat Zenie, of course, slumbers in front of the
fireplace.
And I am astounded, as always, at the blessings in my life.
Fortune circles around my being and I am blessed beyond
all knowing.
Is there a reason for all this and will I ever find out why?
I don't really need to, mind you, it's just my sense of
justice
And wanting to know what I did right somewhere along
the way.
God knows there is a reality of what I've done wrong.
You're here now and that is all that matters
And it makes me want to hold the moment for that much
longer.
But it all slips away and we are left with intentions – good
and true.
But the moment is there for all time
And I will always have the pleasure of knowing its
promise.
There is a love beyond all description
And
It is you and me.

I do believe that there are poems that need no paper
Poetry that can't be written – at least by romantics like me
who grope for words.

I see a most lovely poem every morning
When I look across at your lovely face on the pillow as
you slumber.

I see poetry every evening
Watching you read the paper as we wind down from the
hysterics of the day
And ease into an hour or two of precious together time.

I see an incredible poem when I am waiting for you
And, then, when you appear, my heart literally leaps
And your smile is a poem beyond language.

There was an eternal poem woven into my life
When we met
And we keep adding stanzas
Moment to moment
Day to day.

Thank you for bringing so many loving poems into my life
The poems that need no paper.

Somehow, down a long corridor of years,
I seem to have forgotten loneliness.
The heartache of my early years, at times, still haunts me
Enough to hurt just a little
But the emptiness is gone – a fading memory.

Yes, I know I am blessed
And I try to remember my thankfulness
Each day, every moment
Because I understand there is a fragility here
A shadow that intrudes
Maybe just on the fringes
But there nevertheless.

And so I breathe in my life
Slowly and purposefully
Honoring the forces that have shown me
The incredible love that I share with a wife/best friend
The pride in sharing moments with a remarkable son.

I'm not sure how all this happened
Sometimes I'm not sure how I can show my gratitude
But I have forgotten loneliness.

www.ingramcontent.com/pod-product-compliance
Lightning Source LLC
Chambersburg PA
CBHW031540040426
42445CB00010B/634